BUCK

BASE

by Tyrone Washington

HOUGHTON MIFFLIN BOSTON

Are you a baseball fan? Then maybe you know of Ken Griffey, Jr. He is an African American baseball star. Baseball fans know more black players today.

But in the 1930s and 1940s, baseball was very different than it is today. Back then, over fifty years ago, most baseball fans did not know about African American baseball stars like Buck Leonard.

In the 1800s, white and black players played in the same league. But in 1887, something changed. The National Association of Baseball Players said that black players could not play on major league teams. Black players had to play in different leagues.

For many years, black players played baseball in the Negro leagues. The Negro leagues were like the major leagues. There were all-star games and there was a world series. There were also many good players. But all the players in the Negro leagues were black.

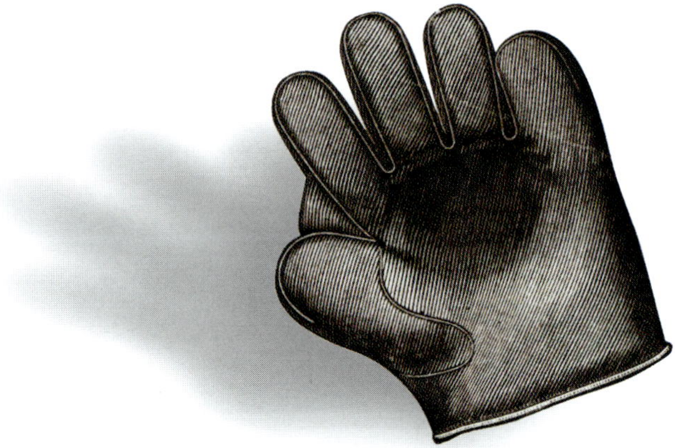

COME SEE

ALL STAR BASEBALL DREAM GAME

— SEE —

LUCIOUS EASTER

who hit a 490-ft. homer into the centerfield bleachers at the Polo Grounds this summer, and other great stars!

ALL STARS ★ ★ ★ ★ ★ ★ ALL STARS

WORLD'S GREATEST NEGRO SPORTING EVENT

INTERLEAGUE CHAMPIONSHIP CONTEST
BETWEEN THE EAST AND WEST

Negro American League All Stars

— VS —

Negro National League All Stars

YANKEE STADIUM
NEW YORK CITY

TUESDAY NITE, AUG. 24, 8:45 P.M.

— ADMISSION —

RESERVED BOX SEATS, $3.00 & $2.00

GRAND STAND, $1.25 BLEACHERS, 60c

Advance Sale at Yankee Stadium, 84 Lenox Ave. — and New York Black Yankees, 127 W. 135th Street

— LINEUPS —

(EAST) NEGRO NATIONAL LEAGUE		(WEST) NEGRO AMERICAN LEAGUE
BUCK LEONARD, Homestead Grays	1st Base	PIPER DAVIS, Birmingham Barons
JAMES GILLAM, Baltimore	2nd Base	RAY NEIL, Indianapolis Clowns
THOMAS BUTTS, Baltimore	SS	ART WILSON, Birmingham Barons
ORESTE MINOSO, N. Y. Cubans	3rd Base	HERB SOUELL, Kansas City Monarchs
ROBERT HARVEY, Newark	RF	JOSEPH COLAS, Memphis Red Sox
LUIS MARQUEZ, Homestead Grays	CF	WILLARD BROWN, Kan. City Monarchs
LUCIOUS EASTER, Homestead Grays	LF	CLYDE NELSON, Cleveland Buckeyes
LOUIS LOUDEN, N. Y. Cubns	C	QUINCY TROUPE, Chicago
WILLIAM CASH, Phildelphia Stars	C	SAM HAIRSTON, Indianapolis Clowns
MAXWELL MANNING, Newark	P	CHET BREWER, Cleveland
ROBERT ROMBY, Baltimore	P	BILL POWELL, Birmingham
DAVID BARNHILL, N. Y. Cubans	P	GENTRY JESSOP, Chicago
JOSEPH BLACK, Baltimore	P	BOB LA MARQUE, Kansas City
PAT SCANTLEBURY, N. Y. Cubans	P	LEFTY VERDELL MATHIS, Memphis
	P	JOHNNY WILLIAMS, Clowns
		KING TUT, COACH

This poster is from 1946. Buck Leonard's name was at the top of the all-star list.

Satchel Paige

Oscar Charleston

Negro league players were not as famous as major league players. But the Negro league had its own stars, and they were as good as major league players. Some were better. The Negro leagues had players like Josh Gibson, Satchel Paige, Oscar Charleston, and Buck Leonard.

Everyone admired Buck Leonard. He was pleasant and easy-going. He had a friendly word for everyone. And he was one of the greatest gentlemen to ever play baseball.

In the Negro leagues, Buck Leonard made baseball history.

Buck Leonard in his Homestead Grays uniform

His name was Walter Fenner Leonard, but everyone called him Buck. Buck was born in 1907 in a small town in North Carolina. His father worked for the railroad. When Buck was a young boy, his father died. His family needed money, so Buck got a job shining shoes.

When he was sixteen, Buck worked for a train company. He also played baseball. He was the star of the baseball team in his town.

In 1934, Buck played first base for the Homestead Grays team of Homestead, Pennsylvania. This was one of the best Negro league teams.

The Homestead Grays in 1941. Buck Leonard is in the first row. He is the third person from the left.

Lou Gehrig

Buck Leonard had a lot of fans. His fans thought that Buck was like Lou Gehrig. Gehrig played first base for the New York Yankees, a major league team. Both players were polite, and both were strong and powerful hitters. But there were even better players on their teams.

Babe Ruth

Josh Gibson

Babe Ruth was the strongest hitter for the New York Yankees. People called him "the Babe." Lou Gehrig was a great player, but Babe Ruth was more famous.

Buck Leonard and Josh Gibson played on the same team. Buck was a strong hitter. But Gibson always hit more home runs than Buck. Gibson hit the ball farther too. He was more famous than Buck in the Negro leagues.

Lou Gehrig and Buck Leonard did not mind being less famous than their teammates. They were great players who could win against other teams.

Buck Leonard tags out a runner in a game in 1946.

Buck Leonard was a hard worker who played well, game after game. Once he played with a broken hand. His team was playing four games against another team, and he broke his hand in the first game. He taped it up and played three more games with the broken hand!

Negro league teams worked harder than major league teams. Major league teams usually played one game in a day. Sometimes they played two games a day—a double header. But Negro league teams often played three games in one day.

Buck also worked hard when he wasn't on the baseball field. Baseball was played only part of the year. So Buck worked when the baseball season was over. He shined shoes, and he worked on the railroad. He worked until the baseball season started again.

Major league players made a lot of money and were famous. Negro league players did not make as much money as major league players. And they were not as famous. During his first baseball season, Buck Leonard made only $125 a month. That was much less money than any major league player. And major newspapers did not write about the Negro league teams. Buck and other good Negro league players had no chance to be national heroes.

Negro League All Stars in 1947

But the Negro league players had a bigger problem. They were not treated very well, because they were black. Buck and his teammates were not allowed to eat in many restaurants. And they could not stay in many hotels. They sometimes slept on the baseball field or in their bus. When the sun came up, they got ready to play. The Negro league players had many problems, but they still loved to play baseball.

Buck played baseball for seventeen seasons. During this time he shone as a star. His batting average was one of the highest in baseball history. To find a batting average, you need to do some math. You divide the number of times a player hits a ball by the number of times he is at bat. A 1.000 is a perfect batting average. Most players do not get a .300 batting average in a season.

Buck Leonard had a batting average of .341. In special games against major league teams, his average was .382. And in 1947, his batting average was .410! When he was 41, his average was .395. That is very high for an older player. Most players in baseball never hit so well.

Buck Leonard runs around the bases after hitting a home run against the Newark Bears in 1943.

Buck Leonard hits a home run in this 1938 photo.

People made up some tall tales about Buck Leonard. One teammate said that one day, Buck hit the ball so far that it flew over the heads of the fans. The ball hit a water tower, and it rained for two weeks! Buck's teammates told these stories because they loved and admired Buck.

In 1938, Buck Leonard and Josh Gibson almost played with a major league team. They met with Clark Griffith, the owner of the Washington Senators. The Washington Senators were a major league team. Clark Griffith knew that Leonard and Gibson were great players. He asked them to play for the Senators. Of course, they said yes!

But they did not play for the Senators. Griffith wanted to get black players into the major leagues, but baseball officials said no. Buck Leonard and Josh Gibson never got a major league contract.

In 1947, things began to change. In that year, Jackie Robinson started to play for the Brooklyn Dodgers. Jackie Robinson was the first black player in the major leagues. He became a hero. He was young and talented. Some people wanted only white players in the major leagues. But Jackie Robinson didn't pay attention to them. Baseball officials saw that Jackie Robinson was a great player and a good person. His courage helped other black players get into the major leagues. Little by little, things changed.

Jackie Robinson was the first African American to sign a major league contract.

Monte Irvin and Larry Doby were two Negro league stars who crossed over to the major leagues after Jackie Robinson opened the door.

In 1952, Buck Leonard was finally asked to play in the major leagues. He was 45 years old. Buck knew he couldn't play as well as younger black players, so he said no. He didn't want to hurt the chances of other black players getting into the major leagues. Buck was always a gentleman and a good sportsman.

Buck Leonard is presented with a plaque honoring his election into the National Baseball Hall of Fame.

In 1972, Buck Leonard got the honor he deserved. He was elected to the National Baseball Hall of Fame.

When he stopped playing baseball, Buck went back to his hometown in North Carolina. He had started out life there shining shoes and had become a great baseball hero.

Buck Leonard died in 1997.